"The purpose of life, after all,

is to live it, to taste experience to the utmost,

to reach out eagerly and without fear."

— Eleanor Roosevelt

HOW
ELEANOR ROOSEVELT
REACHED OUT,
SPOKE UP,
AND
CHANGED
THE
WORLD

ELEANOR
Makes Her Mark

BY BARBARA KERLEY

ILLUSTRATED BY EDWIN FOTHERINGHAM

SCHOLASTIC PRESS | NEW YORK

ELEANOR ROOSEVELT

was feeling a little nervous.

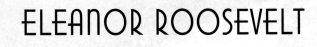

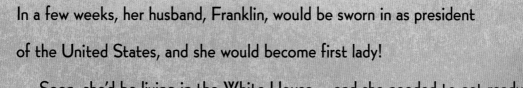

In a few weeks, her husband, Franklin, would be sworn in as president

of the United States, and she would become first lady!

Soon, she'd be living in the White House — and she needed to get ready!

Eleanor told the chief usher that the inauguration ceremonies "must be simple."

In fact, she wanted to serve hot dogs for lunch.

She toured the house from top to bottom, meeting maids and ushers. Cooks.

Butlers. Doormen and engineers.

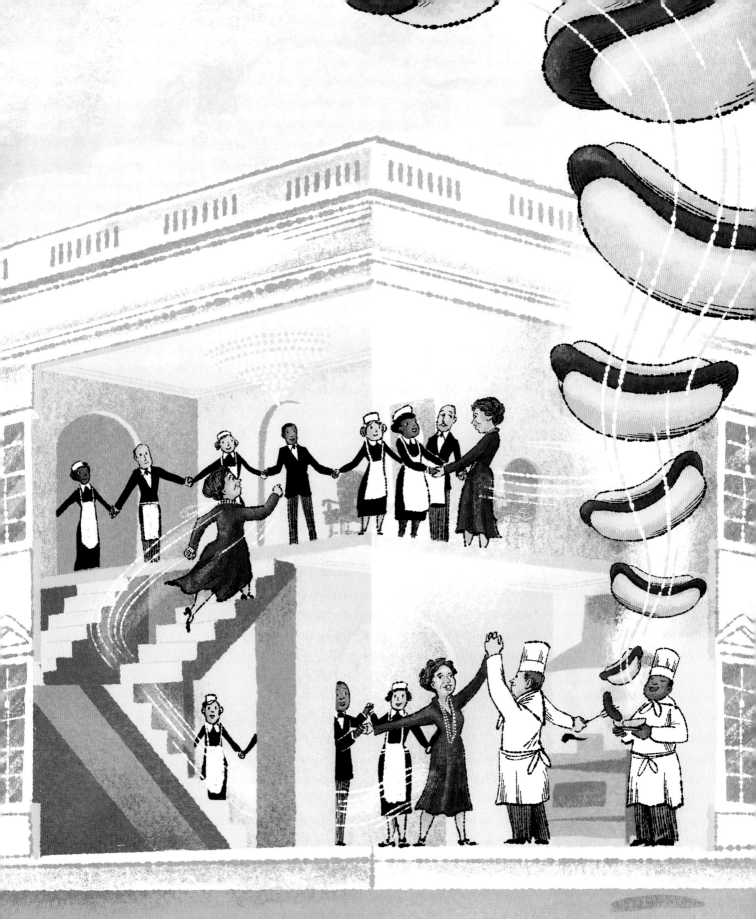

Eleanor was counting on the White House staff to keep things running smoothly.

For as first lady, she wanted more than "merely being hostess" at official functions.

All her life, she'd hoped to "leave some mark upon the world."

When she was young, Eleanor found her "greatest joy" in helping others.

She and Father served Thanksgiving dinner to newsboys who lived on the streets.

With Great-Aunt Gracie, she visited hospitalized children wearing casts and splints that looked very uncomfortable.

And Uncle Vallie took her to decorate a Christmas tree for families in one of the poorest neighborhoods in New York City.

Each experience allowed her to meet people who, she realized, "suffered in one way or another."

Eleanor felt their suffering deeply, for she already knew sadness.

Mother made her feel "too shy" and "solemn."

Father was much more loving, but he drank heavily and was

often out with friends, leaving Eleanor at home, longing for his return.

By the time she was ten, she had learned about loss,

as well — Mother, Father, and her brother Elliott had all died.

For the next several years, Eleanor and her brother Hall lived with their grandmother, who was kind, but *very* strict.

On Sundays, instead of playing games, Eleanor was expected to recite verses and hymns from memory.

She could not lie in bed reading before breakfast — no matter *how* interesting the book she had hidden under her mattress.

Eleanor was not even allowed to choose her own clothes. She had to wear thick, black stockings during long, hot summers in the countryside. If she rolled them down to cool off, she was told that "ladies did not show their legs" and had to roll them back up again.

Eleanor longed for adventure and "desperately" wanted to travel, but Grandmother kept her close to home until she was almost fifteen.

Finally, in 1899, Grandmother decided Eleanor was
grown up enough to attend Allenswood, an all-girls
school in London, England.

There, Eleanor's "real education" began.

Unlike many people at that time, the headmistress,
Marie Souvestre, believed that women could form
their *own* opinions. Her discussions of religion
"shocked" Eleanor "into thinking," and her views
on human rights inspired Eleanor's desire to
work for social justice.

With Mademoiselle Souvestre's encouragement, Eleanor became a leader at the school — so well liked by all the students that on Saturdays, they filled her room with violets.

Eleanor loved Allenswood. But when she turned eighteen, Grandmother declared it "unthinkable" that she not return to New York to enter high society.

For Eleanor, the departure was "very hard to bear." Reluctantly, she packed her bags and headed home.

By now, though, she had formed her *own* opinions about how to live her life.

She obliged Grandmother by going to fancy dances with all the other debutantes.

But she *also* investigated the working conditions of women in garment factories and taught calisthenics to girls in a settlement house.

Most debutantes, she knew, would never step foot in the tenement neighborhoods of New York. But Eleanor wanted to help — and to better understand the lives of people living there.

Eleanor did like *one* thing about being a debutante — it allowed her to get to know Franklin Roosevelt, who was charming and funny. And she liked that he admired her intelligence and her independent spirit. Soon, they were engaged.

After they married and started a family, he became a state senator for New York. Eleanor began to make her own mark in politics by listening to voters' concerns and building connections in the community.

Then in 1921, Franklin contracted polio — a disease that left him unable to walk without leg braces and an arm to lean on.

Eleanor helped him stay active in public life. And when he was elected governor of New York a few years later, she became his partner in the work.

While Franklin toured the grounds of prisons, asylums, and hospitals, Eleanor went inside for a *real* inspection.

She checked to see if rooms were too crowded and if the staff was kind. She even peeked into cooking pots to learn what was bubbling on the stove.

When Franklin was elected president in 1932, he needed Eleanor more than ever.

The country was in the midst of a "tremendous crisis": the Great Depression.

Millions of people were out of work. Banks and schools had closed.

Families lost their homes and farmers lost their land.

How could the president best help?

Who could he trust to reach out to the neediest Americans

and give him an honest assessment?

Why, ELEANOR, of course!

Government, Eleanor believed, should "serve the good of the people," so she encouraged everyone to write to her and share their struggles, hopes, and fears.

In the mornings, she did her calisthenics. She rode her horse, Dot, on the bridle paths of Washington.

Then Eleanor settled into her study. With the help of her assistant, Malvina "Tommy" Thompson, she tackled "a mountain of work" — sometimes receiving hundreds of letters a day.

And if someone wrote a letter she thought especially important, in the evening Eleanor dropped it — along with any memos she'd written — in Franklin's basket for him to read.

Eleanor brought important people to the White House for Franklin to meet: women working for equal rights, students working for a better future, and African Americans working to end discrimination.

But Eleanor wanted to help *more* people — as many as she could.

To do that, she would need to learn about their lives.

So she hit the road, traveling to "unexpected places" that the press found "astonishing" for a first lady. She took the mine train two miles underground to watch four hundred miners dig coal.

She rode in the workmen's cage to the base of Boulder Dam.

She crisscrossed the country,
visiting housing projects, reform
schools, and jails.

Not everyone applauded Eleanor's civil rights work or her efforts to help the poor. Even Franklin sometimes wished she would not push him *quite so hard* to do the right thing.

And some people thought Eleanor should keep her opinions to *herself*.

But that didn't stop Eleanor. Still she gave lectures, held press conferences, made radio broadcasts, and wrote a six-day-a-week newspaper column.

And Tommy took dictation everywhere: in cars, on trains, and even while Eleanor was in the bathtub.

Eleanor's work left its mark on the country — convincing
many Americans that, despite their own hardships
during the Great Depression, they must look out
for others, as well.

But in 1941, just as prospects were brightening,
America faced a new crisis: World War II.

While Franklin oversaw wartime strategy, Eleanor
traveled to the South Pacific, visiting military hospitals
from the Cook Islands to Guadalcanal.

As she stopped by every bed, shaking hands with
the wounded and offering comfort and thanks, she
felt herself "rebel at the horrible waste of war."

FIRST LADY PRAISES
VALOR OF WOUNDED
Tells Men in Navy Hospital at
Wellington, N.Z., They Kept
War Away From Us

The New-York Times.
U.S. DECLARES WAR, PACIFIC
BATTLE WIDENS;
MANILA AREA BOMBED;
1500 DEAD IN HAWAII;
HOSTILE PLANES
SPOTTED AT
SAN FRANCISCO

MRS. ROOSEVELT
VISITS ILL
Sees in Australian
Hospital Men From
New Guinea Front

The New-York Times.

JAPAN WARS ON U.S.
AND BRITAIN;
MAKES SUDDEN
ATTACK ON HAWAII;
HEAVY FIGHTING
AT SEA REPORTED

MRS. ROOSEVELT
FLIES NEAR
FIGHTING
AREA

She returned home more determined
than ever to help build "a peaceful world."

By March of 1945, Eleanor worried about how ill and exhausted Franklin looked.

She prayed he'd "be able to carry on" until there was peace.

All she could do was "make it as easy as possible" for him.

When he retreated to his polio center in Warm Springs, Georgia, to rest,

Eleanor remained behind to continue her work.

She kept in touch with Franklin through phone calls and letters, delighted that he had gained a bit of weight. "Much love to you dear," she wrote. "You sounded cheerful for the first time last night & I hope you'll weigh 170 lbs when you return."

For a few days, it seemed like Franklin

might be getting stronger.

Instead, on April 12, he died.

Eleanor quietly traveled to Georgia to bring his body home.

Just before he was sworn in to replace Franklin as president, Vice President Harry S. Truman had asked Eleanor if there was anything he could do for her.

But Eleanor, who understood the burden he was taking on, had replied, "Is there anything we can do for you?"

Truman soon found the perfect answer.

That December, three months after the war ended, he appointed Eleanor to serve as a delegate to the first meeting of the United Nations General Assembly, an organization founded to foster peace.

And so she was able to leave her mark on the world — leading the committee that created the Universal Declaration of Human Rights: a statement that championed the value and dignity of every human being and captured the spirit of an extraordinary first lady.

CANDID.

COMPASSIONATE.

COURAGEOUS.

ELEANOR.

ELEANOR'S LIFE IN PICTURES

1889

Eleanor at the age of four or five. As a young child, she loved playing with her kitten, puppy, and chickens.

1892

Eleanor around the age of seven or eight, with her brother Hall, father, and brother Elliott Jr. Eleanor and Hall grew especially close after the tragic loss of their parents and brother.

1900

Eleanor spent three years at Allenswood. Many of her classmates became lifelong friends.

1898

Eleanor at about fourteen, the year before she began attending Allenswood in England.

1906

Franklin was Eleanor's fifth cousin, once removed. Here, the year after they married, they pose for the camera: Eleanor holds Franklin's drink and Franklin pretends to work on Eleanor's knitting project.

1919

Eleanor and Franklin with their children. Back row: Anna; James; and Elliott; front row: Franklin Jr.; Franklin; Eleanor; Franklin's mother, Sara, who often helped care for the children; and John. An infant son, the first Franklin Jr., died in 1909.

Eleanor (right) and her friend Esther Lape, one of the founders of the League of Women Voters, worked together on many international and domestic political issues.

1924

As first lady, Eleanor held weekly press conferences for female reporters — ensuring that newspapers continued to employ women during the Great Depression. During her travels, she spoke with local press on a range of issues.

1933

1934

While first lady, Eleanor served as honorary president of the Girl Scouts. Here, she visits scouts in Lexington, Kentucky.

1934

After Eleanor visited Puerto Rico, she worked to improve living conditions there.

1936

Eleanor often toured the projects and programs of the WPA, an agency established by Franklin to create jobs. On a 1936 trip to Des Moines, Iowa, she visited a project to convert a city dump into a park.

Modeling good citizenship, Eleanor votes in the 1936 presidential election in Hyde Park, New York. Franklin was reelected in a landslide.

1936

1936

Eleanor's special fondness for children led her to visit many schools, including this nursery school for African American children. During and after her time as first lady, she worked with civil rights leaders to end racial injustice. Her outspoken efforts were so unpopular in some parts of the country that she received death threats.

1941

Eleanor often met with student activists to hear their concerns and support their efforts to build a better world. Here she meets with students in a leadership training course at the Roosevelt summer home on Campobello Island, New Brunswick, Canada.

1941

Eleanor, her social secretary Edith Helm, and her assistant Malvina "Tommy" Thompson, make plans at the White House.

1943

Eleanor championed the contributions of hundreds of thousands of women in the US Armed Forces during World War II, including those serving at Sampson Air Force Base in Geneva, New York.

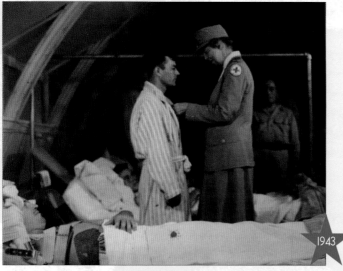

1943

During World War II, Eleanor traveled as a Red Cross representative to visit US forces fighting in the Pacific. Here, she presents a medal to a serviceman in a military hospital.

1947

Eleanor's work as a delegate to the newly formed United Nations brought her deep satisfaction. She considered her contribution to the creation of the Universal Declaration of Human Rights to be her greatest achievement.

1953

In 1936 Eleanor had invited world-famous singer Marian Anderson to perform at the White House. Three years later, when the Daughters of the American Revolution refused to allow Anderson to sing at their auditorium due to her race, Eleanor resigned from the organization in protest, an act that drew worldwide attention. The two women remained friends until Eleanor's death in 1962.

1957

Eleanor and children's entertainer Captain Kangaroo support the UNICEF Halloween program, which continues to provide aid to children around the world.

All her life, even into her seventies, Eleanor traveled widely, carried her own suitcase whenever possible, and worked tirelessly for the causes she believed in.

1960

HOW WILL YOU LEAVE YOUR MARK UPON THE WORLD?

"THE FACTOR WHICH INFLUENCED ME MOST IN MY EARLY YEARS WAS
AN AVID DESIRE, EVEN BEFORE I WAS AWARE OF WHAT I WAS DOING,
TO EXPERIENCE ALL I COULD AS DEEPLY AS I COULD."

From the time she was a small child, Eleanor Roosevelt found her "greatest joy" in helping people. She followed this passion and left her mark upon the world. You can do this, too — because YOU get to choose how to live your life.

Find Your Passion

THINK ABOUT YOUR LIFE TODAY.
- What subjects in school interest you most?
- What are three or four things you love to do outside of school?

START THINKING ABOUT TOMORROW.
- Are there new things you want to try or topics you'd like to learn more about? Write down a few.
- Circle the ones that seem the most interesting and meaningful. Which jobs do you think might be the best fit for you? Why do you think so? Which ones would not be a good fit?
- Brainstorm what you might do if you followed this passion. Is there something you might create or invent? Something you might explore or discover, fix or improve? Write at least two ideas next to each of your passions.

"NOBODY REALLY DOES ANYTHING ALONE. FOR ALMOST EVERY ACHIEVEMENT IN LIFE,
IT IS ESSENTIAL TO DEAL WITH OTHER PEOPLE. . . . IT IS ONLY BY INDUCING OTHERS
TO GO ALONG THAT CHANGES ARE ACCOMPLISHED AND WORK IS DONE."

Eleanor dedicated her life to improving the lives of others. At first, she worked in the community where she lived. But with time, she reached people across the United States and around the world. You can do this, too.

Solve a Problem

THINK LOCAL.
- Brainstorm problems in your community. Are there people who are hungry? Do you know kids who don't have books at home? Is there a park or playground in need of a cleanup? Is there something else that needs attention?
- Choose a problem and find other people who want to help you solve it.
- Plan ways you might solve the problem. Discuss which ideas are best and why.
- Pick a plan and put it into action.

GO GLOBAL.
- List some problems that affect people beyond your community such as too much trash, disappearing habitats, unsafe streets, unfair laws, etc. Do you notice problems that are not getting enough attention?
- What could you do to help with big problems like these?
- Pick one and make a plan. You might write letters to leaders, march for change, start a club, or write or film an interview to draw attention to your cause. Or maybe you'll think of a strategy no one has thought of before!
- Put your plan into action.

"IT IS NOT WISHFUL THINKING THAT MAKES ME A HOPEFUL WOMAN.
OVER AND OVER, I HAVE SEEN, UNDER THE MOST IMPROBABLE CIRCUMSTANCES, THAT MAN CAN
REMAKE HIMSELF, THAT HE CAN EVEN REMAKE HIS WORLD IF HE CARES ENOUGH TO TRY."

FOR MARIJKA KOSTIW — THANK YOU, AGAIN AND AGAIN. — B.K.
FOR MY FAMILY, AS ALWAYS. — E.F.

Many thanks to Sara McCracken, Research Assistant, and Mary Jo Binker, Consulting Editor, for the Eleanor Roosevelt Papers Project at the George Washington University for fact-checking this book.

Thanks also to Brenda Maier, who co-authored the section "How Will You Leave Your Mark Upon the World?"; Virginia Lewick and Sarah L. Navins, Archivists, Franklin D. Roosevelt Presidential Library; Spencer Howard, Archives Technician, Herbert Hoover Presidential Library and Museum; and Shirl Naegle, Collections Manager, Boulder City/Hoover Dam Museum, for research assistance.

QUOTES IN THE BOOK COME FROM THE FOLLOWING SOURCES:

"The purpose…": *Eleanor Roosevelt, You Learn by Living*, reprinted ed. (New York: Harper Perennial, 2016), xii.

"must be simple": Eleanor Roosevelt, *This I Remember* (New York: Harper & Brothers, 1949), 76.

"merely being . . .": (Roosevelt, *This I Remember*, 76).

"leave some mark . . .": quoted in Joseph P. Lash, *Eleanor and Franklin: The Story of Their Relationship, Based on Eleanor Roosevelt's Private Papers* (New York: W. W. Norton & Company, 1971), 85.

"greatest joy": Eleanor Roosevelt, *This Is My Story* (New York: Harper & Brothers, 1937), 13.

"suffered in . . .": (Roosevelt, *This Is My Story*, 27).

"too shy": (Roosevelt, *This Is My Story*, 17).

"solemn": (Roosevelt, *This Is My Story*, 5).

"ladies did not . . .": (Roosevelt, *This Is My Story*, 37).

"desperately": (Roosevelt, *This Is My Story*, 46).

"real education": (Roosevelt, *This Is My Story*, 29).

"shocked . . . into thinking": (Roosevelt, *This Is My Story*, 71).

"unthinkable" and "very hard . . .": (both, Roosevelt, *This Is My Story*, 96).

"tremendous crisis": (Roosevelt, *This I Remember*, 69).

"serve the good . . .": (Roosevelt, *This I Remember*, 6).

"a mountain . . .": Eleanor Roosevelt, "My Day, May 1, 1936," *The Eleanor Roosevelt Papers Digital Edition* (2017), accessed March 13, 2019, https://www2.gwu.edu/~erpapers/myday/displaydoc.cfm?_y=1936&_f=md054321.

"unexpected places" and "astonishing": both, Kathleen McLaughlin. (1936, July 05). "Mrs. Roosevelt Goes Her Way," *New York Times*, July 5, 1936. Retrieved from ProQuest.

"rebel at . . ." and "a peaceful world": both, Eleanor Roosevelt, "My Day, August 30, 1943," The Eleanor Roosevelt Papers Digital Edition (2017), accessed 3/13/2019, https://www2.gwu.edu/~erpapers/myday/displaydoc.cfm?_y=1943&_f=md056580.

"be able to . . .": (quoted in Lash, *Eleanor and Franklin*, 917).

"make it . . .": (Roosevelt, *This I Remember*, 329).

"Much love . . ." and "You sounded . . .": both, quoted in Joseph P. Lash, *A World of Love: Eleanor Roosevelt and Her Friends, 1943–1962* (Garden City, NY: Doubleday & Company, Inc., 1984), 182.

"Is there anything . . .": quoted in Doris Kearns Goodwin, *No Ordinary Time: Franklin & Eleanor Roosevelt: The Home Front in World War II* (New York: Simon & Schuster Paperbacks, 1994), 604.

"The factor . . .": (Eleanor Roosevelt, *You Learn by Living*, 1).

"Nobody really . . .": (Roosevelt, *You Learn by Living*, 123).

"It is not . . .": (Roosevelt, *You Learn by Living*, 158).

"Where, after all…": Eleanor Roosevelt, "10 Inspiring Eleanor Roosevelt Quotes," United Nations Foundation, accessed 4/8/2020, https://unfoundation.org/blog/post/10-inspiring-eleanor-roosevelt-quotes.

"It is quite possible . . .": (Roosevelt, *You Learn by Living*, 133).

Library of Congress Cataloging-in-Publication Data available
ISBN 978-0-545-82612-9
10 9 8 7 6 5 4 3 2 1   20 21 22 23 24
Printed in China   38
First edition, October 2020

Photos on pages 44–48 courtesy of the Franklin D. Roosevelt Presidential Library & Museum.

Edwin Fotheringham's artwork was rendered on an iPad Pro, with an Apple Pencil, using the app Procreate. • The text type was set in Bernhard Gothic SG Medium. • The display type was set in Modified Gothic LT P Regular and Dalliance Regular. • The book was printed on 130 gsm Lumisilk matt art paper and bound at Tien Wah Press. • Production was overseen by Catherine Weening. • Manufacturing was supervised by Shannon Rice. • The book was art directed and designed by Marijka Kostiw, and edited by Tracy Mack.

Eleanor stayed active all her life. Here, she and Fala take a walk near her home in Hyde Park, New York.

1947